NO ACT OF KINDNESS, NO MATTER HOW SMALL, IS EVER WASTED.

AESOP

THE WHOLE WORLD IS A SERIES OF MIRACLES, BUT WE'RE SO USED TO THEM WE CALL THEM ORDINARY THINGS.

HANS CHRISTIAN ANDERSEN

SOURCE: Hans Christian Andersen,
    "The Puppet-show Man" (1851).

WHY NOT GO OUT ON A LIMB? ISN'T THAT WHERE THE FRUIT IS?

FRANK SCULLY

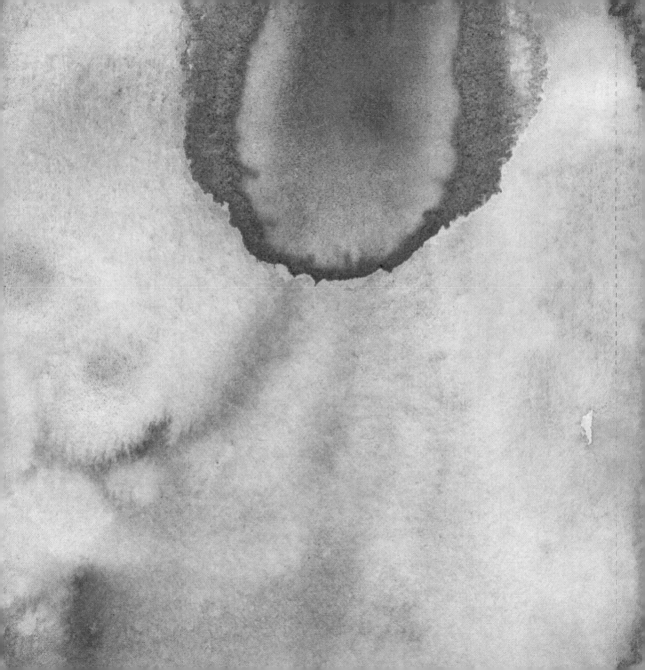

THOSE WHO ARE AWAKE LIVE IN A CONSTANT STATE OF AMAZEMENT.

JACK KORNFIELD

SOURCE: Jack Kornfield, *Buddha's Little Instruction Book* (Bantam, 1994).

LET ME **FALL** IF I MUST. THE ONE I WILL BECOME WILL **CATCH** ME.

BAAL SHEM TOV

LET US

SLOW

DOWN

ENOUGH TO TRULY
NOTICE ALL THAT IS
PRESENTING ITSELF TO US
AS BLESSING.

KRISTI NELSON

JOY
IS THE HAPPINESS THAT DOESN'T DEPEND ON WHAT HAPPENS.

BROTHER DAVID
STEINDL-RAST

SOURCE: David Steindl-Rast, *Music of Silence: A Sacred Journey Through the Hours of the Day* (Ulysses Press, 1998).

LIFE IS NOT THE WAY IT'S SUPPOSED TO BE, IT'S THE WAY IT IS. THE WAY YOU COPE WITH IT IS WHAT MAKES THE DIFFERENCE.

VIRGINIA SATIR

MAKE VISIBLE WHAT, **WITHOUT YOU,** MIGHT PERHAPS NEVER HAVE BEEN SEEN.

ROBERT BRESSON

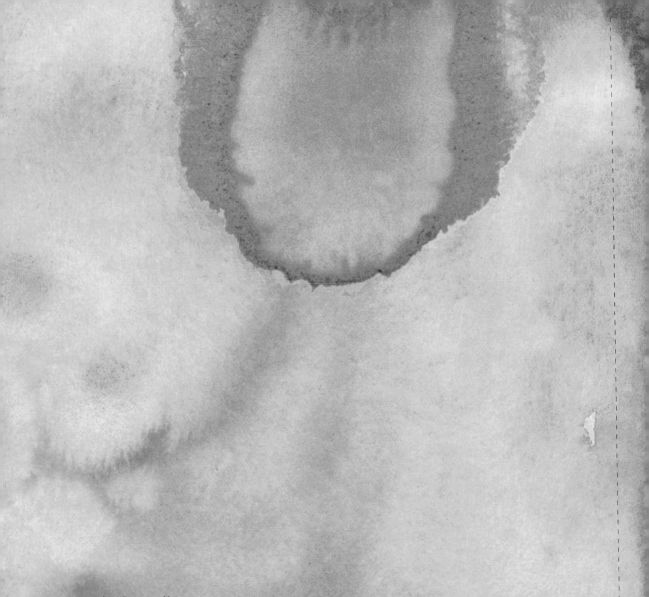

SOURCE: Robert Bresson, *Notes on the Cinematograph* (New York Review Books, 1975).

KNOWLEDGE SPEAKS. WISDOM LISTENS.

JIMI HENDRIX

THE DARKER THE **NIGHT,** THE BRIGHTER THE **STARS.**

APOLLON MAYKOV

THIS
UNIVERSE
IS MUCH TOO BIG
TO HOLD ON TO,
BUT IT IS THE
PERFECT SIZE
FOR LETTING GO.

SHARON SALZBERG

SOURCE: Sharon Salzberg,
  LovingKindness (Shambhala, 2004).

THE MORE I
WONDER,
THE MORE
I LOVE.

ALICE WALKER

SOURCE: Alice Walker, *The Color Purple*
(Harcourt Brace Jovanovich, 1982).

IF I HAD MY LIFE
TO LIVE OVER AGAIN,
I WOULD ASK THAT
NOT A THING BE
CHANGED, BUT THAT
MY EYES BE OPENED
WIDER.

JULES RENARD

WE LOSE TOUCH WITH OUR WINGSPAN WHEN WE HUNCH.

MARTIN SHAW

WHEREVER YOU ARE IS THE ENTRY POINT.

KABIR

SOURCE: Kabir, *The Bijak of Kabir*, trans. Linda Hess and Shukdeo Singh (Oxford University Press, 2002).

NEVER BE SO
FOCUSED ON
WHAT YOU'RE
LOOKING FOR
THAT YOU
OVERLOOK
THE THING YOU
ACTUALLY FIND.

ANN PATCHETT

SOURCE: Ann Patchett, *State of Wonder: A Novel* (HarperCollins, 2011).

One can never consent to creep when one feels an impulse to

soar.

HELEN KELLER

SOURCE: Helen Keller, *The Story of My Life* (Doubleday, 1903).

GRATITUDE IS HAPPINESS DOUBLED BY WONDER

G. K. CHESTERTON

SOURCE: G. K. Chesterton, *The Collected Works of G.K. Chesterton* (Ignatius Press, 1986).

Do your **Little bit of good** where you are; it's those little bits of good put together that overwhelm the world.

ARCHBISHOP DESMOND TUTU

YOU CAN CUT
ALL FLOWERS, BUT
THE YOU CANNOT
KEEP SPRING
FROM COMING.

PABLO NERUDA

THERE ARE
OPPORTUNITIES
EVEN IN THE MOST
DIFFICULT MOMENTS.

WANGARI MAATHAI

SOURCE: Wangari Maathai, *Unbowed: A Memoir* (Alfred A. Knopf, 2006).

TRUST YOURSELF.

YOU KNOW

MORE

THAN YOU THINK YOU DO.

BENJAMIN SPOCK, MD

SOURCE: Benjamin Spock, *Dr. Spock's Baby and Child Care* (Simon & Schuster, 1945).

WAKE AT
DAWN WITH A
WINGED
HEART
AND GIVE THANKS
FOR ANOTHER
DAY OF LOVING.

KAHLIL GIBRAN

SOURCE: Kahlil Gibran, *The Prophet* (Knopf, 1923).

ALL SHALL BE **WELL**, AND ALL SHALL BE WELL, AND ALL MANNER OF THINGS SHALL BE WELL.

JULIAN OF NORWICH

SOURCE: Julian of Norwich, *Revelations of Divine Love*, trans. Elizabeth Spearing (Penguin, 1998).

GRATITUDE UNLOCKS THE FULLNESS OF LIFE. IT TURNS WHAT WE HAVE INTO ENOUGH AND MORE.

MELODY BEATTIE

SOURCE: Melody Beattie, *The Language of Letting Go: Daily Meditations for Codependents* (Hazelden, 1990).

HAPPINESS IS NOT WHAT MAKES US GRATEFUL. IT IS GRATEFULNESS THAT MAKES US HAPPY.

BROTHER DAVID STEINDL-RAST

SOURCE: David Steindl-Rast, *A Listening Heart: The Spirituality of Sacred Sensuousness* (Crossroad Publishing, 1999).

ONE KEY TO KNOWING JOY IS BEING EASILY PLEASED.

MARK NEPO

SOURCE: Mark Nepo, *The Book of Awakening* (Conari Press, © 2000). Reprinted by permission of Conari Press, an imprint of Red Wheel/Weiser LLC. www.redwheelweiser.com.

every
ACT OF LOVE
IS A WORK OF PEACE
NO MATTER HOW
SMALL.

SAINT MOTHER TERESA

SOURCE: Mother Teresa, quoted in *Works of Love Are Works of Peace: Mother Teresa and the Missionaries of Charity* by Michael Collopy (Ignatius Press, 1996).

GIVE
THANKS FOR
UNKNOWN
BLESSINGS
ALREADY ON
THEIR WAY.

NATIVE AMERICAN
PROVERB

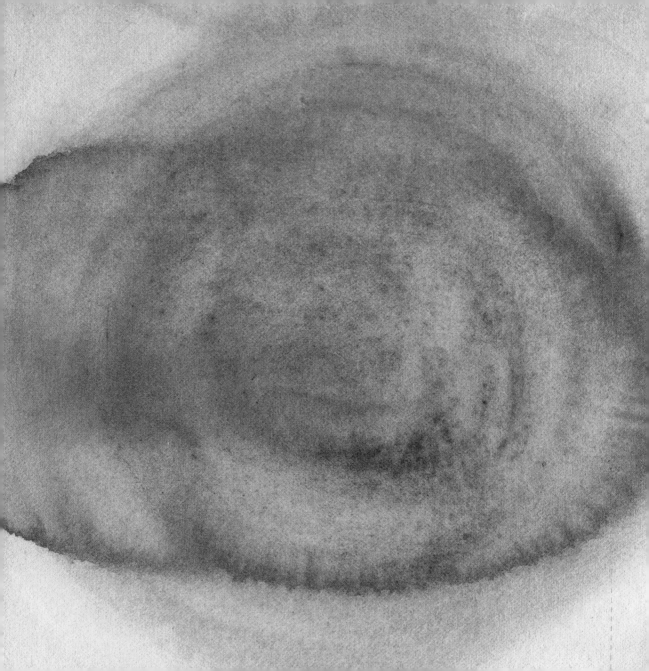

IF THE ONLY PRAYER YOU EVER SAY IN YOUR ENTIRE LIFE IS THANK YOU, IT WILL BE ENOUGH.

MEISTER ECKHART

REMEMBER THAT WHEREVER YOUR HEART IS, THERE YOU WILL FIND YOUR TREASURE.

PAULO COELHO

SOURCE: Paulo Coelho, *The Alchemist*
(HarperSanFrancisco, 1994).

THE SMALLEST
ACT
OF **KINDNESS**
IS WORTH MORE
THAN THE GRANDEST
INTENTION.

OSCAR WILDE

WHEREVER YOU GO, GO WITH ALL YOUR HEART.

CONFUCIUS

DON'T **PLAN** IT ALL. LET LIFE **SURPRISE** YOU A LITTLE.

JULIA ALVAREZ

SOURCE: Julia Alvarez, *In the Time of the Butterflies: A Novel* (Algonquin, 1994).

IT IS A POWERFUL PRACTICE TO BE GENEROUS WHEN YOU ARE THE ONE FEELING IN NEED.

ALLAN LOKOS

SOURCE: Allan Lokos, *Through the Flames: Overcoming Disaster through Compassion, Patience, and Determination* (Tarcher/Penguin, 2015).

ATTENDING
TO LIFE
IS AN ACT OF
LOVE.

KATIE RUBINSTEIN

TREASURE
THIS DAY, AND
TREASURE YOURSELF.
TRULY, NEITHER
WILL EVER HAPPEN
AGAIN.

RAY BRADBURY

SOURCE: Ray Bradbury, *Fahrenheit 451*
(Del Rey, 1953).

GIVE THANKS
for a
LITTLE
and
YOU WILL FIND
A LOT.

HAUSA PROVERB
FROM NIGERIA

Be
HAPPY
FOR THIS MOMENT. THIS MOMENT IS YOUR LIFE.

OMAR KHAYYAM

SOURCE: Omar Khayyam, *The Rubaiyat of Omar Khayyam*, translation unknown.

WHEN WE
GIVE
CHEERFULLY
AND ACCEPT
GRATEFULLY,
EVERYONE IS
BLESSED.

MAYA ANGELOU

SOURCE: Maya Angelou, *Wouldn't Take Nothing for My Journey Now* (Random House, 1993).

Every time we feel SATISFIED with what we have, we can be COUNTED as RICH, however little we may ACTUALLY POSSESS.

ALAIN DE BOTTON

SOURCE: Alain de Botton, *Status Anxiety*
(Vintage, 2004).

ACT AS IF
WHAT YOU DO
MAKES A
DIFFERENCE.
IT DOES.

WILLIAM JAMES

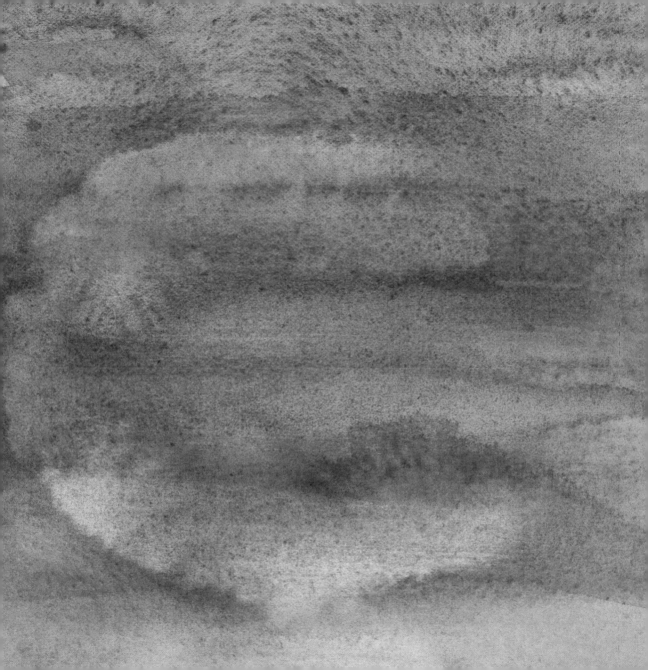

ABUNDANCE IS NOT SOMETHING WE ACQUIRE. IT IS SOMETHING WE TUNE INTO.

WAYNE W. DYER

I WOULD RATHER BE ABLE TO APPRECIATE THINGS I CAN NOT HAVE THAN TO HAVE THINGS I AM NOT ABLE TO APPRECIATE.

ELBERT HUBBARD

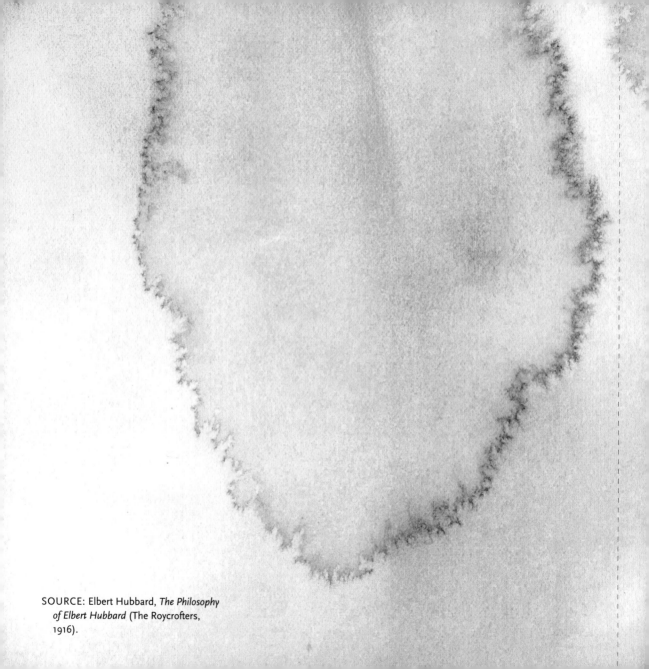

SOURCE: Elbert Hubbard, *The Philosophy of Elbert Hubbard* (The Roycrofters, 1916).

HUMAN BEINGS MUST ALWAYS BE ON THE WATCH FOR THE COMING OF WONDERS.

E. B. WHITE

SOURCE: E. B. White, *Charlotte's Web*
  (HarperCollins, 1952).

I AM, therefore I THANK.

CINDY LUBAR BISHOP

LIGHTHOUSES DON'T GO RUNNING ALL OVER AN ISLAND LOOKING FOR BOATS TO SAVE, THEY JUST STAND THERE SHINING

ANNE LAMOTT

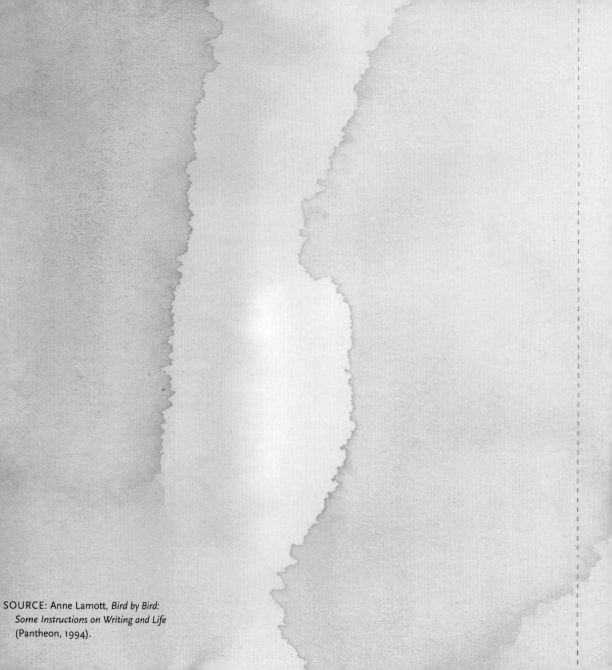

SOURCE: Anne Lamott, *Bird by Bird:
Some Instructions on Writing and Life*
(Pantheon, 1994).

REMEMBER THAT THE HAPPIEST PEOPLE ARE NOT THOSE GETTING MORE, BUT THOSE GIVING MORE.

H. JACKSON BROWN, JR.
& ROCHELLE PENNINGTON

SOURCE: H. Jackson Brown, Jr. and Rochelle Pennington, *Highlighted in Yellow: A Short Course in Living Wisely and Choosing Well* (Rutledge, 2001).

THE
ONLY WAY
TO LIVE
IS TO
ACCEPT EACH
MINUTE AS AN
UN-
REPEAT-
ABLE
MIRACLE.

MARGARET STORM JAMESON

SOURCE: Margaret Storm Jameson,
*The Journal of the National Education
Association*, vol. 48, p. 41, 1959.